792

BERKHAMSTED
COLLEGIATE
SCHOOL

KV-374-026

DATE DUE

GAYLORD			PRINTED IN U.S.A.

Behind Media

Theatre

Catherine Chambers

www.heinemann.co.uk/library
Visit our website to find out more information about **Heinemann Library** books.

To order:
☎ Phone 44 (0) 1865 888066
🖹 Send a fax to 44 (0) 1865 314091
🖥 Visit the Heinemann Bookshop at www.heinemann.co.uk/library to browse our catalogue and order online.

First published in Great Britain by Heinemann Library, Halley Court, Jordan Hill, Oxford, OX2 8EJ,
a division of Reed Educational and Professional Publishing Ltd.
Heinemann is a registered trademark of Reed Educational and Professional Publishing Ltd.

OXFORD MELBOURNE AUCKLAND
JOHANNESBURG BLANTYRE GABORONE
IBADAN PORTSMOUTH NH (USA) CHICAGO

© Reed Educational and Professional Publishing Ltd 2001
The moral right of the proprietor has been asserted.

All rights reserved. No part of this publication may be reproduced, stored in a retrieval system, or transmitted in any form or by any means, electronic, mechanical, photocopying, recording, or otherwise without either the prior written permission of the publishers or a licence permitting restricted copying in the United Kingdom issued by the Copyright Licensing Agency Ltd, 90 Tottenham Court Road, London W1P 0LP.

Designed by Paul Davies and Associates
Illustrations by Keith Richmond
Originated by Ambassador Litho Ltd
Printed in Hong Kong/China

ISBN 0 431 11453 6
05 04 03 02 01
10 9 8 7 6 5 4 3 2 1

British Library Cataloguing in Publication Data

Chambers, Catherine
   Theatre. - (Behind Media)
   1.Theatre - Juvenile literature
   I.Title
   792

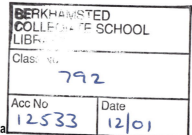

BERKHAMSTED
COLLEGIATE SCHOOL
LIBRARY

Class No.	
792	
Acc No	Date
12533	12/01

Acknowledgements
The Publishers would like to thank the following for permission to reproduce photographs: Arena Ron Scherl p32; Catherine Ashmore pp10, 26, 35; Clive Barda p28; Big Pictures p43; Corbis Dean Conger p30, Kevin Fleming p21, Michael Gerber p32; Robbie Jacks p44; PA Photos p13; Panos Pictures pp8, 45; Performing Arts Library pp4, 25, 33, Sue Adler p6, Clive Barda pp37, 39, 40, Henrietta Butler p12, Simon Cherry p34, Damon Evans p23, Michael Le Poer-Trench pp18, 36,16, Jane Mount Mitchell p9, Jerome Yeats p7; Redferns Graham Salter p19; Robert Harding pp5, 41.

Cover photograph reproduced with permission of Performing Arts Library.

Our thanks to Gordon McDougall for his comments in the preparation of this book and to Martin Brown of Equity for his help.

Every effort has been made to contact copyright holders of any material reproduced in this book.
Any omissions will be rectified in subsequent printings if notice is given to the Publishers.

Contents

Musical Background

Getting it off the Ground!

Musical Skills

Taking Shape

Making it Real

Pulling the Crowds

Any words appearing in the text in bold, **like this**, are explained in the glossary.

Musical Background

Introduction

For thousands of years the performing arts have delighted and challenged audiences across the world. They have entertained and informed societies, and portrayed their dreams and their past. Combining the spoken word, music, song and dance, the musical has done all of this and one other thing – it has dazzled.

This book takes you all the way through the staging of a musical, from its concept to the first night and beyond – charting everything from its production processes and people, to its reviews and rewards. It also looks at how theatre productions in general are staged.

Actors learn to 'play to an audience', trying to draw it into the performance, as you can see in this production of Doctor Dolittle. A live audience reacts differently to each breathtaking performance, and the cast adapts its reactions in return.

What's the big attraction?

Theatre productions range from the flamboyant, sparkling spectacle to the lonely, spotlit **monologue**. They can lift you with stirring speeches and rousing choruses, or they can leave you quietly spellbound with glittering costumes and magical sets. Productions today examine the world around us in new ways, making us think more deeply about the society in which we live. Productions of the past are still performed to packed houses, showing that the range of human emotions, relationships and life's challenges are timeless – only the context changes. In this book we shall be looking at how the musical, whether drama or comedy, set in the present or the past, near to home or far away, is put together as an attractive entertainment package.

Who makes it happen?

The theatre has become a hotbed of talent for writers and actors, dancers and musicians, directors and designers. But it is also a haven for those with practical expertise. The musical in particular has challenged both the imaginations of artists and the skills of carpenters, costume-makers, lighting technicians, make-up artists and computer software designers. We shall be looking at these roles, as well as others within the theatre world, and we shall see how musicals are presented on stage.

Where does it happen?

You can watch a musical or other theatre production either indoors or outdoors – from low down in the **stalls** to high up in the **gods**. We shall be examining the different designs and sizes of **auditoriums** and the acting area of the stage.

Will it last?

The musical has swung in popularity since it crystallized as a **genre** in the early 1900s. Theatre as a whole is facing huge competition from home entertainment systems, such as video and television, and the Internet. We shall be looking at how the theatre industry is trying to make live performance relevant and special – and why it is thriving in some parts of the world and not in others. Theatre is also performed for television and radio and we shall see how this affects live theatre.

*In New York, the bright lights of **Broadway** at night are attractive publicity for a musical production.*

What is a musical?

Musicals combine mostly song and music with dance and the spoken word to play out a plot or a concept (idea). They can be funny or serious, realistic or abstract (see page 27). But what distinguishes them from other similar **genres**?

Porgy and Bess (1935) is operatic in style, but because its score was composed by George Gershwin, who was then seen as an unconventional modernist composer, it was thought of by some as a musical. As Gershwin's music has gained in respect, so the definitions of his work have changed. The score and singing technique are now mostly defined as opera.

Generating a genre

Musicals were first known in the 19th century as 'musical comedies'. They had simple comic plots, played out through song, movement and speech. As the genre developed, the plots became more serious, especially those written by US dramatists in the early part of the 20th century. Song and movement became more sophisticated and were better integrated with the dialogue. Without them, the plot would not now be complete. The overall production came over as slick and seamless. This more professional approach and the weightier topics used led to the genre being renamed just 'musical'.

Musical arguments

However, the theatre is home to many different presentations and combinations of song, music, movement and the spoken word. There has sometimes been hot debate amongst critics concerning the definition of particular productions – whether they are in fact musicals, musical comedies, operettas, operas, comic operas or simply plays with music. Some of the arguments concern how much song there is in relation to dialogue in each production – and whether or not that song is necessary to the plot or characterization. Other debates are largely to do with the quality of the singing or acting. The musical, it is often said, is performed by actors who can sing, while the opera and its related genres are performed by singers who have to act!

Other musical genres

Opera usually plays out serious themes in a serious way. It is mostly sung throughout and performed on the professional stage only by trained opera singers. Comic opera is of the same musical quality as opera, but at times demands more of the performer in terms of acting. Comedy is notoriously difficult to perform successfully. Operetta is lighter in tone than opera and the **scores** are simpler, but the singing style is the same as that of opera.

The musical demands less of the singer in terms of musical quality and voice range than the other genres described. But the performers still have to give a polished singing performance, even if not in an operatic style. The most important consideration, however, is the audience, which for musicals includes many people who would never normally go to an opera. Musical-lovers enjoy the often flamboyant spectacle of the musical as much as the performance elements within it and the plot.

Many modern musicals have become dazzling spectacles, with increasingly inventive themes, sets and production techniques. Musicals such as Starlight Express *involve the audience by members of the cast dancing among it on roller skates.*

Musical roots

Today's musical is rooted in dramatic performances of the past, even as far back as ancient Greece and Rome. In those times, comic and **satirical** works were mimed, spoken, sung and danced by masked actors performing with exaggerated body movements and facial expressions. They were accompanied by musicians and a group of singers known as the chorus.

Around the world

The most famous centre for musicals is **Broadway**, but musical spectaculars are created and produced all over the world. In addition, US productions sometimes open in other entertainment centres such as London's West End, rather than Broadway. In these ways, the musical has become globalized. But other cultures, too, have age-old musical traditions which are still relevant today.

Musical influences

In other parts of the world, the modern musical has now been adapted to local dramatic forms and developments. For example, theatre groups from African countries not only stage their own modern and classical musical performances, but also productions from the USA and Britain. These are adapted to traditional African music and dance forms, or modern musical developments, sometimes using African instruments. The original idea is made more relevant to the African audience. African theatre groups take their performances all over the world, which in turn often influence productions in their host countries.

Australian aboriginal dance and music plays out ancient legends – stories of the dreamtime, when the world began. Heavily made-up performers relate tales of sacred animals and symbolic religious sites.

Ancient and modern

Japan is home to many styles of drama, from classical, through to avant-garde **fringe theatre** and the modern mainstream musical. One of the most important traditional **genres** is noh theatre, which is about 800 years old but is still widely appreciated today. The performances are a highly stylized combination of song, instrumental music and dance and are religious in content, or relate to human beings' struggle with goodness and faith. Noh can be very slow, but its changing drum rhythms reflect the different meanings and emotions within the production. So, too, does the flute, which introduces the most highly dramatic moments of the plot.

Traditional Kabuki theatre, which developed after noh, is much closer to the 'western' musical in that its themes are more about real life, love or historical topics. Both Kabuki and noh theatre have influenced the western musical artform through their stylized use of song, instrumental music and dance. But Japan is always moving on. In the 1960s Japan developed a fresh, lively musical style by integrating pop music and modern dance to play out contemporary themes.

*In a noh performance all the actions, instruments and **props** contribute to the meaning of the performance. Some fan gestures represent feelings such as sorrow in the form of weeping; while others can symbolize weather conditions such as wind or rain. The music and instruments will reflect the meaning of the fan movement.*

A new identity

Early musicals from the last half of the 19th century and the early 20th, were mostly written or influenced by variety, vaudeville, pantomime and by European composers, or those with a European style. After the First World War, which had isolated them from Europe, both America and Britain established their own musical identities. The themes were more contemporary and the melodies and rhythms less restricted in style.

Getting it off the Ground!

What's the big idea?

Thinking of an original idea for a musical is quite difficult. Whatever idea is chosen, it seems as if someone has thought of it before. Who generally thinks of the ideas, and how do they bring them to the stage?

The musical Lion King (1997) is an idea taken from the film of the same name. Both are based on a children's story written over 100 years ago by Rudyard Kipling. With a perfect combination of animals in extremely realistic costume, a boy-hero and themes of loyalty, pride and love, Lion King has been acclaimed also for its score, written by the pop musician, Elton John.

From dream to reality

Well-known composers and **lyricists** are a main source of ideas for musicals. They often work together. Playwrights and even novelists sometimes see an idea working better as a musical than in their own usual **genre**. Occasionally, directors or **producers** from other media, such as film or television, will realize that an idea has potential for the stage, and then will find the right people to write and produce it.

For mainstream shows staged in major theatrical centres, such as **Broadway** and the West End, the idea for the musical is worked into a **libretto** or 'book' (see page 14). Then the **score** is composed, the songs crafted and dance routines worked out. At this stage, part of the show, such as a selection of songs and dance routines, is tried out in a small venue, or 'workshop'. Sometimes this is produced as a kind of cabaret performance – just a string of song and dance numbers, rather than a small bite of the actual plot. Staging a production on this small scale gives a producer and director a reasonable idea of how a bigger production based on the workshop will work. It also shows where rewriting is needed.

Workshops are staged in whatever venue is available, from a community hall to an empty theatre. Only a few, simple sets, lighting schemes, sound effects, **props** and costumes are used. Workshop actors might be well-known performers that the director has their eye on for the main production, or they could be complete unknowns. But the producer and director still want to put on a professional performance, as potential investors for the full show are often invited to it. Workshops are also in the interests of the eventual audience of the final production, as they lead to a slicker and more vivid show. Some Broadway tickets can cost US $90 each, so theatre-goers deserve full value for money!

However, a mainstream musical producer still does not really know that their very expensive production is going to pull in the crowds and please the investors. But they do try to gauge the public's opinion before staging the musical for a long run – maybe a year or more. Until about 30 years ago, a new Broadway production was sent on tour to regional theatres for a 'tryout' lasting from few months to about two years. This enabled the producer and director to study the reviews from local media and then reassess the lyrics, score and dance routines. A lot of rewriting and rearranging then took place. But musicals are now so expensive to stage that most producers preview the show for a few weeks at its main Broadway venue before the true opening night. Although this is a cheap alternative to touring, it does mean that theatre-goers are sometimes subjected to errors that have not been ironed out. It also gives time for rumours about a particular production to circulate, providing theatre critics with a preconceived idea about what they will see on the opening night.

Bad ideas

Some ideas seem good, but still fail to attract audiences. A musical based on Napolean Bonaparte, for example, sounds promising. But an actual production, *Napoleon*, opened in the UK's West End on 17 October 2000 and was forced to close early on 3 February 2001. A well-known UK critic, Michael Billington, said of it, 'Dreams of unending conquest are hardly ideal musical matter.' He suggested that Napoleon's romantic rather than military life would have made for a better show.

Counting the cost

Once an idea is hit upon, a way of putting it on the stage has to be found. A musical is especially expensive to stage, so the **producer** or **theatre manager** has to make sure that enough money is put in to finance the initial costs of the production.

No expense spared

In some countries, such as the USA, the producer is responsible for the financial side of a performance – for buying the rights to the performance, renting the theatre, hiring the actors and staff and handling the receipts. In other countries, this is the function of the theatre manager. On **Broadway** and in the West End musicals can cost several million pounds to produce. This is often more than twice the cost of a normal drama put on in the same theatres.

Why is the musical so expensive? Firstly, it needs not only a writer, called a dramatist, but also a composer, **lyricist** and **choreographer**. Secondly, it needs top-class, versatile actors who can sing and dance to a professional standard. Recording artists and music **royalties** have to be paid. All these artists, plus managers, set and costume designers and technicians, have to be paid their salaries up-front while the musical is in the process of being created and rehearsed. Added to this are huge costs for spectacular sets, lighting effects and publicity. While the production is in progress, **running costs** increase the burden on the budget.

Blast (1999) is one of a number of US musicals to be staged first outside Broadway. Even though the theme is very American, the producers have taken a risk, hoping that the visual spectacle and the mesmerizing music will bring in the audience.

Who pays the price?

A really big, popular production attracts huge audiences over a long period, which helps to cover production costs through the sale of tickets, programmes, **merchandising** and refreshments. It can also attract the sale of film rights, which is the quickest way of recouping the expenditure. But a smaller or less popular production, without the sale of film rights, can take years to cover the investment and make a profit.

Producers or theatre managers attract investment from media and other arts, and from business people. Well-known hit musical writers, such as Andrew Lloyd-Webber, have little trouble attracting funds and often help to finance productions themselves. Most central and local governments also support the performing arts to some extent through public funding, known as subsidies, although this has decreased in the last decade, especially in the USA and ex-communist East and Central Europe. Many theatres also have a system of private funding through arts' foundations or supporters' groups.

Many musicals have made huge amounts of money. But some theatres try to run on a non-profit-making basis. Their motive is to produce less commercial works, bringing innovation in terms of content, performance and production techniques. Variously known as **fringe theatre**, experimental theatre and, in New York City, Off Broadway, they often end up relying on the state or on donations from benefactors.

Andrew Lloyd-Webber, creator of many successful musicals, now owns several London theatres. He does not want to fill them all with musicals, however, but he has hinted that some might become venues for musical traditions from other parts of the world. It is hoped that this will help attract a new type of audience to keep the theatres profitable.

On the job

A theatre producer or manager needs to know all about finance in the theatre world, theatre production and how to attract both investors and audiences. They have to work well with others and respect their expertise. A good start would be to help produce a school or community play, taking responsibility for one area, such as hiring **props** or costumes. There are courses in theatre finance and management.

Writing it down

A huge range of ideas can be translated into a musical. But first the idea has to be written down. Some musicals are almost pure song and dance; others have more dialogue.

The starting block

A brilliant idea for a musical still has to be shaped into a seamless plot with a really good storyline behind it. This 'play' aspect of the musical is known as the **libretto**, or 'book'. It is the solid framework that holds together the **score**, the songs and whatever dialogue there may be. Importantly, the book stops the musical from being just a string of numbers and dance routines. The creator of the 'book' is the librettist, who has to ensure that the plot and characterization lend themselves to song and dance. He or she must create characters that the audience cares about, while the action must be varied and not too predictable, to hold the audience's attention. The recent trend in musicals is for minimal dialogue and plentiful song and dance, so the work of the librettist has become less prominent and some would say, less appreciated. But trends come and go, so this could all change in the future.

Most mainstream musicals are now written in two acts, and traditionalists sometimes make the first act quite a bit longer than the second, as in a lot of play-writing. The librettist uses the first act, whatever its length, to set the scene, build up the plot and subplots and familiarize the audience with the characters. At the end of this act, some storylines might end in a cliffhanger, while others could leave unresolved questions about certain characters.

These and other devices are used to attract the audience back to their seats for the second half. In musicals, the second half is usually extremely dramatic and powerful. It builds up into a crescendo of dance and song, and pulls together the main plot and sub-plots. A strong, catchy theme song and chorus, used perhaps earlier in the musical come into their own in this grand finale.

Catchy choruses

The choruses of many songs written for mainstream musicals have a certain familiarity about them. This is because they have been written to a format. In the format, the chorus is four lines long, with each line divided into eight musical bars. The first, second and fourth lines contain the same melody while the third is a complete contrast, known as a release or bridge. This style is known as the AABA format and has produced many very popular numbers. The sample opposite does not follow the AABA 'rule', like some of the less conventional musical productions.

As you can see from the small sample of a fictitious musical opposite, the ensemble of cheerleaders sing a chorus or refrain. The chorus is taken from a song sung earlier in the performance – one which will also be repeated in rousing fashion at the end. This is typical of the way in which major songs are used in mainstream musical productions, linking together parts of the plot or roles of specific characters throughout the performance.

BRETT: [gasping for breath, holding out hand] 'Shake?'

KENSAL: [gasping for breath, putting hands behind back] 'Shake? With you? You *fake*!'

[Exit]

[Enter cheerleaders for both teams]

SNAKESTON'S CHEERLEADERS [singing]:

It's tickertape day! Tickertape day! Tickertape day!
Steal? We *stole*!
Slam dunk? We *whammed* dunk!
Beat ya? We *slaughtered* ya!
It's tickertape day! Tickertape day! Tickertape day!

WRECKTON'S CHEERLEADERS [singing]:

It's bitter fate day! Bitter fate day! Bitter fate day!
Steal? You *snatched*!
Beat us? You *cheated* us!
Slam dunk? You *shammed* dunk!
It's bitter fate day! Bitter fate day! *Bitter fate day*!

This is part of a scene from a fictitious musical called 'Tickertape Day', about two basketball teams' quests for success. The spoken text and stage directions are laid out just like an ordinary play, and there's a sung chorus. This is set to different types of music throughout the musical, depending on the mood required. The rhythm of the word 'tickertape' is danced and drummed throughout in a similar way. Dance routines for musicals are learned and rehearsed separately, so these would be represented on a working script just as cue-ins.

Technical tips

The musical has many devices for achieving tension and high drama, through expressive movement, voice and instrumental music. Carefully worked-out pauses and stillness can create suspense. But so, too, can cut-and-thrust dialogue – short, snappy lines spoken or sung in short verses alternately by different characters. They can be whispered and breathy, or gradually build up into a climax of tension or excitement.

Let's dance!

Oklahoma! (1943) paved the way for more elaborate musical choreography. It was choreographed by a collaboration between Agnes de Mille and Jerome Robbins.

Dance is a spectacular element of the musical. The **choreographer** has to consider the director's interpretation of a scene and the mood of the music to create a well-integrated **routine**. They also have to cast the dancers, who must be able to perform the styles of dance required.

Planning positions

Choreography begins once the music and songs have been composed. A choreographer has to be aware not only of the limitations of the dancer, but also the dimensions and layout of the stage, and the position of any non-dancing performers. Modern musical spectaculars often extend the stage by dancing in the aisles of the **auditorium**, or on the apron – part of a stage that extends into it. This enables the choreographer to create movements that interact more with the audience. Steps and raised levels, known as rostrums, make the choreography seem more three-dimensional and interesting.

Making moves

The choreographer has to collaborate with the director, **musical director**, set designer and costume designer. He or she has to bear in mind that dancers sometimes have to sing as well as move, so some sequences have to be less challenging than others. As well as this, singer-dancers must be audible at all times, which affects the dancers' position on stage unless the performers are wearing radio microphones. The style of dance has to be right for the period and place in which the musical is set, and the subject matter. For example, some sequences in *Oklahoma!*, which you can see in the picture opposite, lent themselves to movements based on country folk and barn dancing. *Cats* (1981), on the other hand, used both ballet and modern dance techniques, but with close attention to lifelike cat movements.

Creating choreography on computers has made dance routines evermore spectacular, as the choreographer is able to push movement to more accurately-known limits. Not only can the computer show three-dimensional animated figures from many different angles, but it can also outline the dimensions of the stage. *West Side Story* (1957) transformed the role of dance in musicals, for the whole piece was danced throughout. *A Chorus Line* (1975) and *Dancin* (1978) are two well-known examples of danced musicals that followed it. Choreographers such as Jerome Robbins, Bob Fosse and, more recently, Tommy Tune elevated the role of dance in the musical. They led to the increasingly influential role of **director-choreographers** in the production of the American musical.

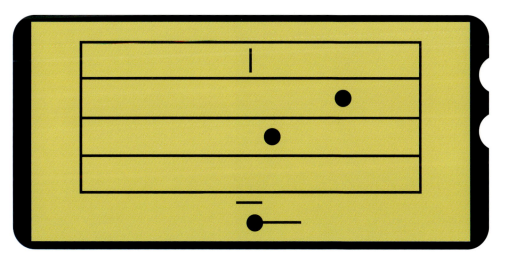

Dances can be read! A dance can be written down in a special notation, using stave lines, just like music. This is Benesh Notation, which was developed in the 1950s. The lines and dots represent, from the top, movements of the head, shoulders, waist, knees and lower leg. The dancer in the notation shown here would have a raised head, outstretched arms and be standing on one leg!

On the job
Most dancers begin by training in classical ballet at a local school, and then in a dance or drama college. Modern dance, tap, Latin American and different folk dancing techniques are all useful techniques for the musical. A good singing voice is also necessary. Involvement in local productions can be fun, but professional training is where the real skills develop.

Making music

And now to the main point of a musical – the music! Once the composer has created the **score**, the **musical director** auditions the musicians.

Using music

Musicals are known for their haunting melodies and catchy choruses. The composer has to make sure that the music created is right for the style of the lyrics and dialogue, and the time and place in which the story is set. The performers rehearse the songs before any other part of the musical – movement, dance and spoken word all have to follow from the music.

Many composers use variations of a theme tune to tie the story together. Minor theme tunes are used for the main characters, to help the audience identify their roles and to alert them when a particular character is going to enter the stage. Music is also used to achieve effective contrasts of mood and to slow the pace of events or speed them up.

How does it sound?

Most mainstream musical productions now use radio microphones to reach the audience. Some purists feel that this is against the spirit of live theatre, but it does allow for a more sensitive interpretation of both music and dialogue. Also, while theatre music is traditionally played live, increasingly it is recorded. In 2000, an entirely recorded musical, *Contact*, was mimed throughout by its energetic performers.

Music is not the only sound that you will experience in the theatre. Those rolls of thunder and pounding hoofs all have to be created live or taken from pre-recorded CDs and cassettes. The special effects are recorded onto a single CD or tape and each sound is marked on a cue sheet. During performance, the **assistant stage manager** calls the cues and the technicians play the effect required to its correct volume and duration.

Stephen Sondheim, born in 1930, has created some of the most successful and musically moving productions of all time. Unusually, in 1962 he wrote both the music and lyrics for A Funny Thing Happened on the Way to the Forum.

During a performance, the sound is controlled from a technical box, facing the stage. The sound crew operate a mixer, to fade the sound in and out and control the volume and duration of all the sound sources, whether live or recorded. The sounds are fed first into an amplifier, which increases the volume. They are then broadcast through large speakers set on each side of the stage, with smaller, portable ones placed so that the music or effect can come from a particular direction as necessary.

Sound effects can be pre-recorded or played live. This special percussion instrument is used to make a sound like a lion roaring.

On the job

A musical director needs to be a trained musician, knowledgeable about most instruments, voice and broadcasting. A useful way to start is to help create and organize music and sound effects in a school production. It is necessary to be able to understand what the play or the musical is trying to achieve and to work well with the cast and the director.

Acting it out

Actors in musicals have to be very versatile, professional performers of the spoken word and song. With dance now dominating many modern musicals, they also have to be skilled and trained as dancers, and very fit. However, acting skills are still at the heart of the performance.

Keeping in character

Whether singing, dancing or speaking, the musical performer has to act and react according to the role they are given. They also have to relate to other characters and their stage environment in a particular way. So even when an actor dances, they have to dance with the feeling and mannerisms of their character. While singing, their voice and body language have to be consistent with the role. To do this requires total concentration and a lot of rehearsing, until the part becomes natural.

In addition, the actor has to be aware of, and relate to, other cast members, the space on stage and the **props**. If, for instance, they are acting in what is supposed to be their own sitting-room, then they have to relate to it as if it is – being relaxed and comfortable with it. If, on the other hand, they are acting a timid person in an unfamiliar space, then actions and reactions should be consistent with the uncertainty that this brings.

Mind and body

In drama school, actors learn how to get under the skin of characters in order to feel and behave as they do. But they also try to learn as much about themselves as possible. This is so they can empty out their own personalities and instinctive reactions, making way for that other person to take over.

Actors have to have as much control over their bodies as their brains. But they also have to be relaxed. Today's techniques for achieving these seemingly opposite sensations include warming-up exercises to loosen both muscles and mind. Flexing individual muscles and then releasing them relaxes each one. It also reminds the actor of the workings of each individual part of the body, which they will later be able to remember and control as they wish. Breathing exercises help concentration, relaxation and breath control, which affects both movement and **diction**.

Actors have to work well with many different people, and they have to learn to trust the other actors on stage. In drama school this is learned through simple, but demanding, exercises, such as allowing fellow students to lead them around blindfold, or letting themselves fall into someone's arms. Actors also have to work well on their own, learning lines. Songs, with their rhythms and rhymes, are often easier for the brain to absorb than **prose** or dialogue. Sometimes actors tape the lines and listen to them at home while they perform other tasks.

The best method?

Getting to the heart of a character and trying to understand what motivates them is known as 'method acting'. It was pioneered by the Russian actor and director, Konstantin Stanislavsky (1863–1938). He developed his ideas while working in the Moscow Art Theatre. By the 1930s method acting had found its way to the USA. Variations of 'the method' are now used all over the world.

A young girl is beginning her audition. For auditions, actors prepare a couple of pieces of their own choice, which they perform in front of the director and assistants. For musicals, actors need to show that they can sing and dance. One recent survey found that almost 50 per cent of actors work in their chosen profession for less than three months a year.

Sounds good

The voice is the most powerful instrument of communication on stage. Performers seem to use it effortlessly, but, like any other part of the body, it needs to be trained and kept in trim. Before a musical performance, the voice captain will do warm-up voice exercises with the chorus (see also page 29).

It's all under control

A performer, whether singing or acting, not only has to get across someone else's thoughts, but also has to recreate the mood dictated by the script or the lyrics and the director's interpretation of them. So, as with the body, the voice has to be extremely versatile, but well disciplined.

A tense body gives a tense voice. So relaxation exercises are an important start to **pre-performance** preparations. This means tensing and then relaxing face muscles and tongue, and exercising vocal chords with a series of sounds from deep down where the diaphragm lies (the muscle above the stomach and under the lungs). Breathing from the diaphragm makes the voice deeper, stronger and more controlled. In tense moments, the voice is expelled well above the diaphragm, giving a throaty, weaker, wavering tone.

Sounds easy

In a musical, songs often carry the plot forward. So, it is very important that every word is heard clearly. Whether singing or acting, the performer breaks down language and mood into different sounds, tones and volumes, which they can recall at will. Vocal exercises might begin with vowel sounds, using varying lengths and strengths, and either voicing them or breathing them. The voiced ones make a more echoing sound in the voice box, while the breathed, voiceless ones are softer – more breathy. It is the difference between, for instance, a short, sharp 'a' and a long, whispered, breathy 'aaah'.

There are also two main types of consonant to run through: plosives and continuants. Plosives, such as p, t, b, d, g, k and ch, are spoken not as they are in the alphabet, but as if they are beginning a word: bus, tin and so on. Plosives begin with a build-up of air in the mouth and explode when released. These can be breathed or voiced, too. Continuant consonants such as m, n and ng (as in the word 'singing') have a relaxed hum about them and are not exploded. These can be practised with different lengths and strengths, too, such as a short, soft 'm' or a long, enthusiastic 'mmm'.

It's only words

How does the performer apply all these exercises and control to the words of the play or song? **Scores** and scripts are carefully written – even the punctuation means something and cannot be ignored. Commas, colons and dashes indicate that the actor has to pause. But for how long? The mood of the speech and its context – its overall meaning within that particular part of the play – all help the actor to decide. Words that are continually repeated in a speech, or for the role as a whole, indicate to the actor that they are important. He or she should probably put stress, or emphasis, on them. Emphasis and intonation – the way the voice rises and falls over each phrase of the script or song – add to the understanding of the performance.

*Actors practise expression and **inflection** by saying single words several times, but emphasizing different syllables and voicing them with varying strengths. The same thing can be done with sentences, stressing different words and repeating them with contrasting moods: calm and panic; love and rage; contentment and frustration.*

Musical movie stars

Sometimes, movie stars are engaged for the lead roles on the world's major stages, as they are certain to boost ticket sales. Almost before they do anything else, the **producer** or manager of a mainstream musical will try to engage a superstar for the opening weeks. An audience is often interested to see whether screen actors have stagecraft as well as screen technique. Many arts critics see this as an expensive gimmick and would prefer to see stage actors in lead roles from the start of the production.

The final actor

So what are all those exercises in body, voice and self-awareness for? They are designed to make the final presentation to the audience as believable as possible, so that it becomes drawn into the performance. And when this magical state is achieved, the audience performs back. It is, as many actors say, 'the final actor'.

Two-way traffic

Actors under bright lights often cannot see the audience sitting in the dark. They can hear it, though – not only the applause and the laughter, but also the grunts, the murmurs, the whisperings and the shufflings. It is this sound plus an inexplicable electricity between the **auditorium** and the stage which creates the relationship between actor and audience. And it is different with every performance, affecting cast members in the way they time their lines and their pauses, in their **inflection** and even their mannerisms, the way they dance and the way they sing. Any actor who is unable to 'feel' their audience bulldozes through their performance. And however beautifully spoken the lines, however graceful the gestures, their role is dulled by their inability to communicate it.

When actors are unable to sense the mood and reaction of the audience, it is usually because they are nervous or insecure in their role. These feelings are picked up and reflected back from those watching, creating a downward spiral. The credibility of the role is jeopardized and sometimes, too, are the performances of other actors, whose own rhythms and roles are disturbed.

Casting the audience

As well as reacting to an audience, the actor sometimes has to actively engage it, using the audience as cast members. Lines that require this must be spoken genuinely, as if the audience is a real character in the play. This, however, is really difficult with such a sea of faces or abyss of blackness in front of the actor. So he or she must sector the audience. This means that they focus their lines on a set of individuals dotted around the mid-rows of the auditorium – or several small patches of space, if the audience is difficult to see. The actor then moves from one individual to another with their eyes and movements, just as if they were talking to a group of people on stage.

The manner in which the actors play to the audience is partly in reaction to its response. But it can also be pre-planned by the director. This is especially true of the musical. Dancers and singers often engage the audience by performing directly to them, and even among them as the action spills out into the auditorium.

Musical movies

Successful musicals are often made into movies, but the actors that attracted the theatre audience are not always picked for the film role. In 1999 the *Phantom of the Opera*, a success on both **Broadway** and in the West End, was voted the best and most profitable musical of the 20th century. Part of its success lay in the star performance of its first 'phantom', the UK actor Michael Crawford. But the film company wanting to make it into a movie intends to choose a younger, well-known film star. A campaign was launched in the USA to support Crawford's bid to star in the film version.

Producers and directors know that an audience is attracted by the looks and fame of actors playing the star roles in a mainstream musical, as well as skills and temperament. But some musicals have made actors famous, too. Here you can see a production of The King and I, which was first staged on Broadway in 1951. It made a star out of Yul Brynner, who played the king.

Taking Shape

The right direction

The director's role is huge – he or she has to pull the whole production together and must enable all those involved to achieve a believable and innovative performance.

Pulling it together

In theatre, the script is the basis of every decision that the director makes. In the case of the musical, so is the **score**. The director's interpretation touches every other aspect of the production – how it looks, how it sounds, how it feels. For the musical, the director co-operates with the **musical director**, **choreographer**, set designer, lighting designer and costume designer to create the right atmosphere for the work. In fact, there is usually so much to do in putting on a musical that there is often more than one director. In recent years there has been a move toward upgrading the role of the choreographer, who in a dance-dominated musical has taken on a directorial position. At all times the director has to work within a given budget, co-operating with the **producer** or **theatre manager**, who is responsible for finances (see page 12).

*Here the director helps to create the tension between the two actors by positioning them in a certain way. The director also has to make sure that **props** and make-up work with the overall look, sound and feel of the production.*

What does it mean?

The interpretation of the script and the director's guidance to all those involved in the production are vital to the success of a performance. Interpreting means finding the central meaning and mood of the script and understanding the characters. If the writer is still alive, and particularly if the script is new, then the director usually works with him or her, to understand what motivated the plot and characters.

A new interpretation of an older work or a traditional tale, however, might involve linking it to current political events, relating it to the character of the region in which the play is being performed, or the type of theatre company playing it. In November 1999, for example, the UK's Strathcona Company, with its troupe of disabled actors, staged *Hood*. The play is based on the legend of Robin Hood, but in this production Robin is a young man with learning disabilities. A director could also set the play far in the past or in the future. Musical **revivals** allow the director also to reinterpret songs and instrumentals. They can change the number of singers, the quality of the voices, the number and type of instruments, and the tempo (speed) of the song to give a totally different sound. A **director-choreographer** can also reinterpret dance numbers. Part of the director's success in all this lies in choosing performers who are able to understand his or her interpretation and yet add their own individuality to the roles.

No direction

Not all theatrical productions are director-dominated. In some societies, such as those found in many parts of Africa, the audience expects actors, singers, dancers and musicians to automatically perform traditional pieces in a particular way, and with known styles of make-up and costume. The interest lies in how well the performers execute the known format.

In Europe and America, some companies have also rid themselves of the director – and the writer! The actors use methods of **collective creation** to move the plot and the roles forward on their own, following only the bare bones of a script.

The idea is that the whole theatre group creates the play and develops the roles. Together, they research, write, discuss and improvise, leading to a production that emphasizes relationships between the group members as much as what they are trying to express. Collective creation emerged in the late 1950s–1960s. One of the most well known groups is the San Francisco Mime Troupe (1959) which developed a reputation for its performances in public parks. These incorporated song, mime, dance, musical accompaniment, comedy and even juggling into each performance, rather like the old vaudeville and variety shows on which musicals were partly based.

Choosing the style

Musicals can be spectacles designed to 'take you out of yourself', to entertain rather than to make you think. They bear little resemblance to real life. But many modern musicals seek to represent the everyday experiences of 'ordinary' people in particular political or social settings – a trend begun by American musical writers and directors. A good example of this is the award-winning musical *Rent* (1998), which deals with issues such as homosexuality and power within relationships.

On the job

A director needs to know about all aspects of theatre production and be able to understand and analyse scripts. They have to understand what motivates actors, singers and dancers, so that they can get the best out of them. Above all they require a lot of patience and courage. It is possible to start as an assistant director for a school or community production. There are courses in theatre direction, although some directors begin as stage managers or even actors.

27

Practice makes perfect

Aslick performance by talented performers leaves the audience admiring them for their art. The truth is, though, that while good performers stamp their own individuality on their role, the director often dictates their every expression, their every move.

Making it move

The **director's technique** describes how the director plans and instructs performers in the way they express the text, and in their gestures, positioning and movements around the stage. For a performance that is only staged for a week or so, the director has little time to spend on it. But a long-running play or musical takes several weeks of rehearsal to perfect. Each rehearsal concentrates on a different aspect of the show. But one of the main purposes is to work out how the performers move around the space they are given. There has to be a point to everything that happens on stage.

The director only brings in an actor when they can make a contribution to the drama, and only keeps an actor on stage for as long as he or she gives value to the scene.

*Every tiny motion or action performed is noticed by the audience. So, too, is the 'woodenness' of a performer who doesn't move or do **business**. Getting movement right is both important and difficult, and all actions mean something or serve a practical function. Even stillness has to be planned and have a point to it.*

Getting it right

In a musical, no dance ensemble or chorus would be able to function without a dance captain and a voice captain. These two roles are filled by very experienced dancers and singers. They are the first to learn the dance routines and songs, help coach the understudies (or 'swings' as they are sometimes called) and take warm-up sessions. When a performer is ill or injured, the captains make sure that all the positions in the routines and songs are filled properly. Sometimes, captains take a break from performing themselves so that they can study how the other dancers and singers are executing their performance. This is to make sure that routines and songs remain accurate and technically tight. The **choreographer** and **musical director** just couldn't do without them!

The director plans movement and business at the **blocking rehearsal**, which shows performers where they will stand and move and, especially in the musical, makes sure that actors and dancing ensemble do not get in each other's way or obscure the audience's view! The floor of the rehearsal space is often marked with tape to show the actors where they should be positioned. At this stage the performers use substitute costumes and **props**. But real props are used if the actor needs practice in using them. Performers now do a **run through** of the whole performance without the script. The director and performers concentrate on making it seem real, slick and confident.

In the **technical rehearsal**, the stage manager helps the technical crew to cue in sound and effects. Following this, the **dress and tech** rehearses the roles of the performers and the crew together. It's nearly there! The **dress rehearsal**, sometimes with invited guests, is the very last chance to get it right!

Technical tips

Movement is the term used when performers move to different positions on the stage, either horizontally or vertically. It also includes the way an actor moves – running, jumping, and so on. Inherent movement is demanded in the script as part of the plot. Imposed movement is usually added to enrich the role or the look of the scene.

Business is the term used for the manipulation of objects as the performer moves or speaks. Necessary business is an important part of the plot. Imposed business helps to reinforce the characteristics of a part or relationship.

This is a diagram of a conventional stage. The positions, such as upstage right and centre stage, are referred to by actors and directors alike throughout rehearsal and are written on the script.

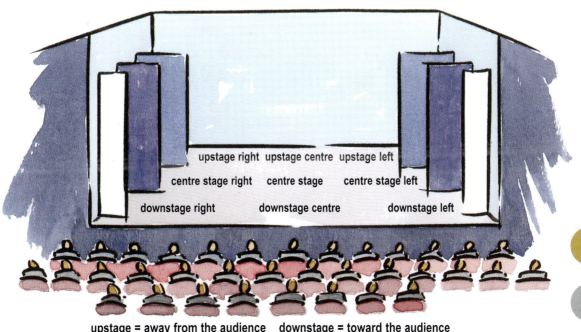

upstage right   upstage centre   upstage left

centre stage right   centre stage   centre stage left

downstage right   downstage centre   downstage left

**upstage = away from the audience   downstage = toward the audience
left and right = toward the left or right as you look at the audience**

Around the theatre

The conventional stage – grand and imposing, with lavish, gliding curtains – is probably what most people have in mind when they think of a theatre. But there are many different kinds of space in which actors work, and many ways in which they use it.

Here you can see the orchestra of a traditional theatre performing in the pit, between the stage and the first rows of seats. In some musicals, the musicians actually perform on stage and are part of the story.

Play space

Performance space can be anywhere. It is the way it is arranged and used that is important to a production, and this, too, is in the hands of our busy director. The manner in which space is planned, or not, has meaning in itself. So, too, does the position of the audience, which, as we have seen on page 24, is an integral part of the production. Whatever space is used, it must conform with fire and safety regulations, which restricts its design and use.

Performances of many traditional musical dramas in parts of the world today, such as Africa, Australia and the Pacific Islands, often take place outdoors, with the audience gathered or dotted around. This arrangement is mirrored in some built theatres, which only have a central open space. The actors decide on the area on which they will perform, and the audience then plans their own seating around it. Known as the promenade design, it makes every performance fresh, as movement has to be altered slightly every time and so does the physical relationship with the audience. But there are other, more formalized spaces, as you can see on the right. Sometimes even these will be extended, the director using the aisles of the **auditorium** for entrances and exits.

'All the world's a stage ...'

For some the magic of the theatre lies in its ability to transform totally the illusion from one scene to the next behind those deep velvet curtains. And it was largely the invention of the proscenium arch theatre about 350 years ago that allowed this to happen. The audience, arranged in rows, is like a fairly distant spectator who has to be drawn into the performance.

The thrust stage involves the audience more in the production and enables those sitting on each side of the stage to see something slightly different.

Theatre-in-the-round offers a huge variety of interpretations of the performance, and a close relationship between actor and audience.

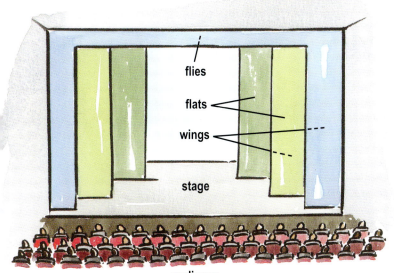

flies

flats

wings

stage

audience

In the proscenium arch theatre, different scenes, often painted on wooden-framed flats (see page 32), are pulled out from or hidden behind the **wings** or up above the **flies**.

In the thrust stage the use of scenery and **props** is restricted, as there is only a backdrop to provide alternative environments. Sometimes, though, an arch is attached to the thrust stage, making scenery and the relationship with the audience more varied.

audience

audience

audience

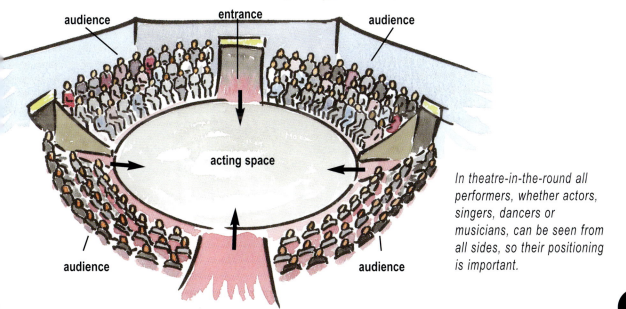

audience

entrance

audience

acting space

audience

audience

In theatre-in-the-round all performers, whether actors, singers, dancers or musicians, can be seen from all sides, so their positioning is important.

Making it Real

A world of its own

Many musicals are spectacular events with elaborate scenery and **props**, while other performances have no scenery or props at all. Some of this is determined by the budget, but many directors choose flamboyant or simple set designs for a reason.

On the set

A set is the creation and arrangement of every piece of scenery or object on stage for a particular scene. The style of the set and the way in which the properties (props) are positioned is determined by the director and achieved by the set designer, carpenters and painters. Together, they plot the props and lighting for each scene on diagrams of the stage, which are drawn to scale and marked like architects' plans.

Sometimes, a piece of the set needs to be emphasized so that it adds to an actor's performance and the meaning of a production. A raised door with steps leading up to it, for instance, helps to **build the entrance** or **exit** of a character. Many larger theatres are able to vary the visual aspect of the performance by using partitions, trap doors, **corner traps**, revolving stages and **inner stages**.

Most sets for musicals are designed to draw the audience into a fantasy – to make it really believe the plot and the characters involved. This is known as representational theatre, and is easiest to design in proscenium arch theatres (see page 30), where all the mechanics of the set can be hidden away. Presentational theatre, on the other hand, does not attempt to hide the untidy bits – the lighting, the wires hanging down, the scaffolding and so on.

Materials used for making scenery must be easy to craft into different shapes and lightweight for swift scene-shifting. Flats and screens are used to make walls and partitions. All the scenery has to be fireproofed before it can be used on stage.

On the job

A set designer needs to provide the right environment for a production within a limited space. They also need a good imagination to visualize how a three-dimensional set will look under different lighting schemes. Building techniques and materials have to be studied, too. The ability to work with other people is vital, especially the director and set builders.

Here, in the musical Fiddler on the Roof, *the house has to be lightweight, but also strong enough to hold the fiddler. Heavy scenery is hard to move on and off stage in the limited time available between scenes.*

Performing with props

Props help to give character to a role. During a performance, actors' personal props are carried with them on stage, while hand props are kept on a table behind the scenes, where they are given out by and handed back to an **assistant stage manager**. The way the actor uses props reflects the role being played and the emotions that the character is feeling at any one time. If, for example, an actor uses a computer keyboard, then his or her joys and frustrations are reflected by the way they tap or pound the keys.

Lighting it up

Lighting was once used on stage just so that the audience could see the actors. It is now an important part of theatre design, creating the mood of a scene or character. Musicals often use spectacular lighting effects to complement sparkling scenery and costumes. Sometimes, as many as 800 lights are used.

Light fantastic

Lighting is an essential ingredient of the musical spectacle – it changes shade and shape; it even moves. The set designer and lighting crew work with the director to create light and shade that will best suit the rest of the design, the costumes and make-up. Lighting up actors and creating the right shadows, or no shadows, requires lamps in front, behind and at the sides of the performers.

Floodlights are groups of very bright lamps set in frames called battens. Floodlighting, either from above or as footlights, is used to illuminate the whole, or most, of the stage in an even light. The lights are either set on the floor or attached to steel grids high above the stage. Each individual lamp is about 20 times more powerful than a normal light bulb, so it can get very hot performing under them, especially in an energetic musical.

Fresnel lamps are used for a more subtle effect. These give a soft edge to the light. Several of these lamps can be overlapped to cover a wide area of the stage. When it is necessary to highlight actors and important parts of the set, the Profile Spot Lamp (Leko) is often used, as it has a harder edge to it than the Fresnel. Spots can be covered with aluminium shutters, called gobos, to focus the light into a particular shape.

Sometimes the director wants the audience to concentrate on a very small area of the stage, or just one actor. This can be done by pin-spotting, which is created by fixing a long hood onto a Profile Spot Lamp (Leko), as in this picture.

Set supremo!

Josef Svoboda (born 1920 in what is now the Czech Republic), is one of the most influential set, costume and lighting designers of modern times. He has included laser and kaleidoscope lighting, moving, reflecting mirrors, and new projection systems to combine live action with filmed images on stage. His innovations have had a dazzling effect on lighting design for the musical.

During **technical rehearsals** and performances, lighting is controlled from the lighting booth. All lighting is wired into a **dimmer box**. In large, modern theatres this is connected to a computerized **piano board**, which controls both light and sound. In smaller theatres, manual piano boards use **sliders** to fade light in or out, up or down.

On the job

Most theatre crews working behind the scenes are trained in specific technical skills, such as carpentry or electrics. Before getting these qualifications it is a good idea to help behind the scenes in an amateur or school production to see how different effects are created and how they are cued into the performance.

Looking the part

Dancers, singers and actors all have to look right for the part. They also need to move around effortlessly under hot lights. Costumes therefore have to be designed very carefully for both the performers' comfort and the critical eye of the audience.

Correct costumes

The director, set designer and costume designer have to work together to achieve the right look for the period, the mood and the colouring of each scene. The right costume helps the actor to **get into character**, as it reminds him or her of their role, and the time, season and place in which they are performing. Costume also tells the audience the age and social status of the character, and possibly even their job.

Some of the most difficult costumes to make are those for animals. The enchanting costumes for the musical Cats (1981) allow the performers to flex their bodies in a cat-like fashion.

All these functions mean that the set and costume designers have to research the parts to make the final effect look authentic. Even the correct underwear must be found to match the outerwear, especially for period costumes. This is because the underwear affects how the overgarment sits on the body, and together they help to influence the authenticity of the performer's movements. The costume designer then sketches ideas for each part, which the director has to approve. Then accurate measurements of each actor are taken and the garment is made.

Made to measure

Lighting and costume have to be planned so that coloured lights do not make the costumes look dreary, or almost invisible against the backdrop. Light reflects well from shiny and sequined costumes, used in many musicals. But coarsely woven or knitted fabrics reflect less light and so look dull and limp, which is fine for a medieval peasant scene, for example.

The costume designer has to design and cut the costumes with movement and comfort in mind. These days, modern synthetic fabrics are made to stretch yet keep their shape. Accessories such as hats, scarves and bags must not be too heavy and must be firmly attached so they do not fly off the body when the performer is dancing or moving fast. Gloves, socks and other items of clothing must be easily removable if that is what is required.

Looking in the wardrobe

The wardrobe is a theatre company's collection of clothes and accessories and is the responsibility of the wardrobe manager. In small theatres, most costumes are reused, although not necessarily in their original form. A collection of cheaply-bought – often second-hand – trimmings, such as lace, fur, heavy rich curtain material, buttons, buckles and belts, are all used to create 'new' costumes for different periods and roles. So, too, are colour dyes. Sometimes costumes cannot easily be made, in which case they are borrowed or hired, as are any wigs or hairpieces that cannot be adapted from the wardrobe.

Masks have been a feature of theatre for thousands of years. One of the most famous masked figures of the modern musical is the 'Phantom of the Opera', shown in the picture.

On the job
A costume designer needs practical dressmaking skills and knowledge of a wide range of materials, from cloth fabrics to plastics. They also need to be able to work with other people, to be very imaginative and to work within tight budgets.

Putting on the grease

The final part of the actor's costume is make-up. Sitting in front of the dressing-room mirror applying the tints and the powders helps to prepare the performer for their part. It transforms the actor into a character. Why and how is it done?

Why put on the make-up?

A person's natural skin tone looks too flat on stage and does not define the features: the eyes, nose, cheekbones and chin. The face and its expressions shrink behind the impact of the costume and scenery. So make-up is necessary, even to create just a natural appearance. With today's strong stage lighting, however, a 'natural' make-up is kept very basic and subtle. Slightly brighter, bolder make-up, especially on the cheeks and around the eyes is used, for example, for a festive scene or an 18th-century ball, to reflect the atmosphere of a special occasion.

Musical spectaculars, with their bright, glitzy costumes, require brighter make-up so that the face does not recede. The actor begins making up by cleaning and toning the skin. Then they apply foundation, shading to give shape to the face, then cream eye shadow. The whole face is then powdered and the actor continues with powder eye shadow, mascara, rouge and lip colour.

To age an actor, the first step is to cover the face in a paler, slightly grey or yellow shade of the actor's own skin colour. The actor then screws up their face to see where lines naturally occur, and then darkens, deepens and extends them with a sharp colour stick. Dark tones are used over and under the eyes and in the hollows of the cheeks. Talcum powder is an age-old greying agent for the hair!

What's in the kit?

Many actors make themselves up for stage performances when there are no special requirements, unlike TV and film, which employ professional make-up artists. The contents of an actor's typical basic make-up kit is outlined in the table below. There is a variety of materials, because each kind gives a different texture when it is applied to the skin. The kit needs to contain different shades of most items. As well as this, there is an aquacolour palette, which is a multi-purpose 'paintbox' with very bright colours for the face or eyes. The kit should also contain brushes of different sizes and shapes, cotton wool, tissues and damp sponges. Many actors also include false eyelashes, eyebrows, moustaches and beards in their box or bag.

For the face	For the eyes	For the lips
Cleanser and toner	Powder eye shadows	Lip gloss
Cream foundations	Cream eye shadows	Lipsticks
Cake foundations	Eyeliners	Lip liners
Translucent powders	Mascaras	Colour sticks
Cream highlighters	Eyebrow pencils	
Grease sticks	Colour sticks	
Grease tubes		
Rouge powder		
Rouge creams		

Here, a professional make-up artist is applying special make-up. Strong make-up is applied for characters with unusual features, such as animals or vampires. Large noses, ears or other characteristics are specially constructed from latex or plastics and stuck on the face with adhesives. Foundation blends the joins and makes the feature look like part of the face. These added pieces are called prosthetics.

Technical tips

☆ Dark shades along the sides of the main features shape the face, while highlights along the ridges of the bones make the features stand out.

☆ Rouge should be applied with a large soft brush, and for a basic make-up used subtly just to mark out the contours of the cheekbones.

☆ A liberal dusting of translucent powder is applied to set the make-up. This is especially important if oil-based greasepaint is used, otherwise the skin can look too shiny.

Pulling the Crowds

Spreading the word

It is close to the opening night and the stars' faces are pasted on billboards all over town. This is the work of the publicity crew who have been promoting the production and preparing for the opening night.

Creating good news

Even before the first rehearsals have begun, the publicity manager and assistants work with the **producer** and director to present the production in the best possible light. Once the lead roles have been established, the publicity manager and assistants are able to promote the production through the star performers, and any well-known director, writer, composer or **choreographer**. By liaising with their agents, the publicity manager can plug the show through TV and radio interviews, or magazine features.

*Posters outside the theatre and in the **auditorium** make theatre-goers aware of forthcoming attractions as they queue up to see a performance.*

The manager and assistants write material for newspaper stories and advertisements, magazine articles and websites concerning the production and any interesting **pre-performance** details. These can include an introduction to a budding star performer, visiting musicians from overseas, or a completely new treatment of a **revival**. They also prepare all other promotional literature, such as leaflets and the programme.

In large cities throughout the world, neon lights shine around the outside of the theatre. While the most popular shows are nearly always sold out on the night, the lights attract tourists to the box-office to book for another showing.

First night

The glamour and the celebrities who attend the opening night are all part of the well-oiled publicity machine. Stars from film, theatre and television are invited by the publicity manager to help boost the first performance with this impromptu fashion show. They are hoping that this will attract media attention and the public.

Inside the theatre, the **front-of-house** staff, organized by the house manager, are there to see that everything runs smoothly. Programme assistants wait in the **lobby**, ready to hand out the programmes to the guests, although at future performances they will be selling them. Ushers guide the audience to its seats, while box-office attendants hope that the event will encourage the public to buy tickets for further performances. After the show, an army of maintenance staff cleans up the theatre, the lobby and the rest rooms.

Technical tips

'Scaling the house' is the expression used for working out how much theatre tickets should cost. In a large, conventional theatre, **boxes**, and **stalls** in the mid-front area are usually the most expensive. Seats at the sides and back are cheaper, while **upper balcony** seats are the cheapest of all. Free passes, or 'comps', are given to people who have given goods or services to the production.

Paying for publicity

Everything has to be paid for, including publicity. The programme is usually financed by advertisements, which are often placed by local firms. Just a few of these can pay for the printing costs, with the rest helping to cover other publicity materials. The programme always thanks companies and organizations which have lent or given **props**. This is an advertisement in itself for the donors and is often a substitute for payment for their goods or services. The programme also usually contains a synopsis of the plot and information about the main actors.

The verdict

Musicals are usually spectacular – spectacular successes or spectacular flops! The press is ruthless to any production that does not come up to the expectation of all the publicity that preceded it.

News and reviews

Press night, often held after the **dress rehearsal**, is make or break time for any theatre production. The next day, pictures taken from the photocall before the dress rehearsal will be publicly displayed in newspapers all over the town or city. So, too, will the opinions of media reporters and theatre journalists in the review sections of newspapers and on breakfast TV and radio entertainment slots. A production can close within weeks or even days following poor reviews – and can stay for many years if the verdict is good. New York's **Broadway** theatres are particularly nervous about criticism. The public pays a lot of money to see a Broadway show so they take notice of reviews, both positive and negative.

Many musical-lovers surf the Internet for write-ups, quizzes and interactive discussions about particular productions or the musical **genre** in general. Topics include the merits of individual lead performers and issues such as, 'Should Broadway shows be less noisy?'. The theatre industry has to take notice of all these opinions.

Is it right? Is it decent? Is it fair?

Theatre was once considered improper – a bad influence on all those who took part in it or watched it. Over the centuries writers and performers have struggled to make it a respectable form of entertainment. Nowadays, part of the reviewer's job is to advise the public whether a production is suitable for families, and whether any violence, nudity and so on is of artistic merit or really essential to the plot. On the whole, reviewers are keen to be seen as broadminded, and often promote the value of these elements within a production. However, the public does not always agree. Religious musicals especially, such as *Joseph and the Amazing Technicolour Dreamcoat* and *Jesus Christ Superstar,* come under fire from independent monitoring groups and religious and family organizations.

Theatre takes place in a confined space, and is not subject to public broadcasting laws as are radio, television and film. So censorship is rare. This is also due to the way in which theatre is run. In many countries where theatres are not publicly financed, theatre companies obtain licences to perform in suitable premises. Licensing laws usually cover matters such as health and safety, but are not allowed to legislate for a show's content and production values.

Theatre for all?

Is the theatre open and just to all sections of society? For black writers, **producers** and actors, the musical more than any other genre has encouraged both stereotyping and the genuine development of black theatre. As early as 1903 an influential musical comedy and the first full-length production written and acted by African Americans was Cook's *In Dahomey*, performed both on Broadway and in the West End.

Precious prizes

In the early 20th century, the American composer George Gershwin and his brother Ira, the **lyricist**, put the musical comedy on the map by receiving the international Pulitzer Prize for Drama for their work, *Of Thee I Sing*. Since then, the musical has increasingly been rewarded in terms of prizes and status as a genre.

Every musical writer and director, composer and lyricist wants to win at least one of the 21 categories of Tonys – the USA's most prestigious stage awards. These were named after Antoinette Perry (1888–1946), actress, writer and director, and one-time chairman of the League of New York Theatres and Producers, which gives the medallions.

In many countries, the theatre trade unions, such as Britain's 'Equity', hold major awards ceremonies. The awards reflect the opinions of people actually working in the industry, and so are highly valued by the winners.

Actors are pleased by the recognition for their work that an award means. Here four actors pose with their awards at the 1999 53rd annual Tony ceremony at the Gershwin Theatre in New York.

The future

The major cities of the world have no trouble drawing in the crowds for the musical. But with competition from home entertainment systems, television and the Internet, what has theatre in general got to offer? Where does its future lie? Will it last?

A big challenge

Theatres outside the world's great capitals are struggling. Many are being closed down. Theatre is increasingly criticized for being **elitist** in terms of both cost and the types of show produced. How can the young, the disadvantaged and those living outside our capital cities become the next theatre-goers?

Targeting young people through theatre workshops encourages participation and creates a desire to see others perform. In many countries, professional performers and production staff help out in children's theatre and local amateur productions. This raises the overall standard and profile of theatre.

Festivals are probably one of the best advertisements for live theatre, and attract huge audiences each year. Some, such as the Edinburgh Festival and Brazil's Fete Mambembao, are host to hundreds of dance troupes and drama groups from all over the world.

Kora players from Senegal, Mali and The Gambia in West Africa perform ancient stories of great rulers and past glories. Each generation of performers updates the past, linking it with present social and political events. They play and sing using new styles. This is why they are still going strong.

Film, television and radio versions of famous dramas encourage a new audience to the theatre. Regional theatre companies often try to engage at least one well-known theatre, TV or film star for each production, to attract bigger audiences. They also engage overseas troupes and companies to add variety to the year's programme. But does the problem lie in the type of show produced? The way ahead for the musical perhaps lies in more productions based on youth culture, like *Blast* (see page 12).

Widening the horizons of theatre means attracting a new audience in an innovative way. London's New Globe Theatre is bringing the past into the present by staging Shakespeare's plays in a replica of one of the theatres in which they were originally performed. Looking to the future, the theatre now also has an underground museum, opened in February 2000. With information, interactive games and even a Shakespeare karaoke, it is attracting a new audience. The success of the interactive devices is a sign that some of the public wants to participate more in theatre, something which the musical has always tried to develop.

More than a musical

Some musicals leave such a lasting impression that their songs are performed in many other contexts. One recent example of this was the UK's *Beautiful Game* (2000), set in Northern Ireland. Its strong theme of peace and reconciliation led the former US President, Bill Clinton, to invite a member of the original cast, Josie Walker, to perform one of the show's songs at his end of Presidential term gala at the White House.

Glossary

assistant stage manager   the person who assists the stage manager in preparing for the performance; during the performance he or she checks that all the set, props and actors are ready

auditorium   the audience's seating area in a theatre

blocking rehearsal   when actors practise their positioning and movement on stage, which have been worked out by the director

box   small raised audience booths at the sides of the auditorium

Broadway   the area in New York City famous for its many theatres and dazzling theatre productions

build an entrance   when the director creates a focus on actors entering the stage, maybe by using a flight of steps descending from the wings

build an exit   when the director creates a focus on actors exiting the stage, maybe by using a prominent exit point, such as a flight of steps into the wings

business   an actor moving props as he or she speaks, such as stirring a cup of coffee or sorting papers

choreographer   the creator of dance movements in a production

collective creation   plays written and directed by a group rather than by individuals

corner trap   a type of trapdoor placed behind the front curtain at the side of the stage – found usually in older theatres

diction   pronouncing and projecting words clearly so that they can be easily understood

dimmer box   a box into which all stage lighting wires are connected; its circuits can control the flow of power to each lamp and therefore dim it or brighten it

director-choreographer   a choreographer (see above) who also directs the performance

director's technique   the way a director instructs the actors to express the text in voice, gesture and movement

dress and tech   a rehearsal for technicians and actors in costume

dress rehearsal   the final full rehearsal with all the costumes, sound effects, music and lighting

elitist   performances that are only meant to be understood by, and available to, privileged people

flies   the place above the stage where scenery or even actors are lifted on and off the stage by pulleys

fringe theatre   unusual performances played in unconventional places, such as parks, warehouses and on the streets; the plays are often put together through collective creation (see above)

front-of-house   all the parts of the theatre used by the audience, including the auditorium, refreshments room, box office and so on

genre   a category or group; in this case, the musical is a genre of stage performance

get into character   when an actor tries to fully understand the character's motives, way of life, and so on in order to play the role effectively

gods   the highest seats in the upper balcony of the auditorium – usually the cheapest part

inflection   the way an actor varies the way his or her voice rises and falls

inner stage   the area at the back of the stage, sometimes concealed, and also known as the discovery space

libretto   the text or book of words for a play, musical, opera or operetta

lobby   the area outside the auditorium where the audience waits before they take their seats

lyricist   the writer who creates the words, or lyrics, for songs

merchandising   goods made in association with a particular production as a money-spinner and as part of the production's promotion

monologue   an actor delivering a performance on his or her own

musical director   the person in charge of all music performed or played back on stage

piano board   a computerized lighting control box to which the dimmer box (see above) is wired

pre-performance   the production activities that take place before the opening night

producer   in the USA, the person responsible for the financial side of a production, for obtaining the rights to stage it, and so on

prop   object placed on stage, or carried or held by an actor

prose   ordinary sentences; spoken words that have no regular rhyme or rhythm

read-through   the first rehearsal of the musical or play in which the actors just read through and discuss their parts with the director

revival   a new production of a previously-performed play or musical

routine   a sequence of dance steps

royalty   money paid to the composer of a piece of music or the writer of a play, for example, every time it is perfomed or broadcast

running costs   costs that occur during the whole run of the play, such as staff costs, hire of props, theatre maintenance and so on

run through   whole acts or full performance rehearsed in one go without the script

satire   a play or musical that gives a witty slant on life's problems, the bad decisions of politicians, corruption and so on

score   the written music of a performance

sliders   sliding buttons that control and fade lighting and sound

stalls   the rows of seats set directly in front of the stage in a theatre's auditorium

technical rehearsal   a rehearsal for technicians to make sure that they cue in lighting and sound effects at the right time and with the right intensity; also to make sure that the equipment works properly

theatre manager   in the UK and some other countries, like a producer (see above), the person responsible for the financial side of the production, for obtaining the rights to stage it and so on. Also the person responsible for managing the day-to-day running of the theatre itself.

upper balcony   the higher balcony in the auditorium

wings   where actors make their entrances and exits at the side of the stage, hidden by flats or curtains

Index

Titles in the *Behind Media* series include:

Hardback   0 431 11450 1

Hardback   0 431 11452 8

Hardback   0 431 11463 3

Hardback   0 431 11461 7

Hardback   0 431 11460 9

Hardback   0 431 11462 5

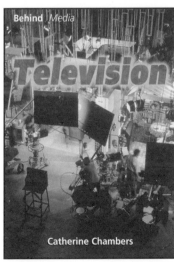

Hardback   0 431 11451 X

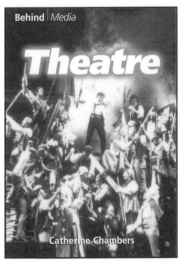

Hardback   0 431 11453 6

Find out about other Heinemann books on our website www.heinemann.co.uk/library